Reincarnation Blues
And other Poems

by Frank Thomas Smith

Art work: Cover, back cover, illustrations
Celina MacKern

Reincarnation Blues
And other Poems
Copyright © 2023 by
Frank Thomas Smith.

All rights reserved. No part of this book may be reproduced in any form or by any electronic or mechanical means including information storage and retrieval systems, without permission in writing from the author. The only exception is by a reviewer, who may quote short excerpts in a review.

This book is a work of fiction. Names, characters, places, and incidents either are products of the author's imagination or are used fictitiously. Any resemblance to actual persons, living or dead, events, or locales is entirely coincidental.

Cover Artworks:	Reincarnation Blues
Artist:	Celina McKern
Year:	2023
Material:	Watercolor
Where:	Artist's collection
Other Illustrations	Celina McKern

Frank Thomas Smith
Visit his website at
https://southerncrossreview.org/

Cover designed by James D. Stewart

Printed in the United States of America
First Printing: November 2023

Anthroposophical Publications
https://AnthroposophicalPublications.org/
https://Anthro.Pub/

ISBN-13: 978-1-948302-55-5 Paperback
978-1-948302-56-2 eBook

Table of Contents

Reincarnation Blues 1
  Canto I 1
  Canto II 3
  Canto III 5
  Canto IV 7
  Canto V 9
  Canto VI 11
  Canto VII 13
  Canto VIII 15
  Canto IX 17
  Canto X
    (The Brothers Karamazov – a review) 19
  Canto XI 21
  Canto XII
    Love's Lament 23
Christ Comes to Skopelos 26
The Three is One 28
  Forward 29
  The First Circle 30
  The Second Circle 31
  The Third Circle 32
The Actress 34
Bad Advice 36
Midnight Christmas 38
The Initiation 40
Carioca Crack 42
Chess and Cheese in Crete 44
Found and Lost in Crete 46
The Daughter of the Sun 48
Exile's End 51
The Expatriate 52
Falú in Zurich 54
The Return of the Gaucho 56
The Last Judg(e)ment 59

Libra	60
Mireya	62
The Oak	64
Occult Science	66
Old Friends	68
The Parting	70
The Pickpocket	72
The Professor of Philosophy	75
Sonnet to Love	77
The Tall Trees of Brooklyn	78
Missing The Point	81
The Return of the Magi	82
Celestial Traffic Jam	84
The Working Stiff	87
Ultimate Questions	89
Twin Pillars of Wisdom	90
The Drone Cometh	92
Translations	94
Credo	94
Prologue in Heaven	
from **FAUST** by Johann Wolfgang von Goethe	98
About the Author	105
Other Books	107

Reincarnation Blues
Canto I

'Twas a distant dance ago,
More real than a writer's rhyme,
Longer than you'll ever know,
Little to do with what's called time.

If a century or two is time at all,
Then dream of it before you go,
Then dance to it spring and fall,
For when you go, you'll never know.

You think there's nothing at all to lose.
You better think again, baby,
And heed the Reincarnation Blues:
That death's a-dawning and that ain't maybe.

It all depends on certain stuff
You did or didn't do this time,
Being good is not enough
Nor partaking of Bread and Wine.

Is there time still to repent
For all the bad you did to others?
For all the gifts to yourself you sent
Instead of your sisters and your brothers?

It still depends on all the stuff
You did or didn't do last time:
Being good is not enough
If love in life is left behind.

You think there's nothing at all to lose.
You better think again, baby,
And heed the Reincarnation Blues:
That death's a-dawning and that ain't maybe.

Reincarnation Blues
Canto II

I'd really like again to live,
Not this long, but longer still.
Would I then have more to give,
With more to feel but weaker will?

There was a time in northern climes,
When I thought and felt and sought
And willed, but failed in troubled times;
And countless were the lies I bought.

Then in seasons southern born,
Fluttered the spirit's broken wing,
Or was it an angel in female form,
Whose beauty made the cosmos sing?

When I ask myself what
I'm doing here I shake my head.
It's neither cold here nor hot,
The feeling I have is one of dread.

For what if I'd traveled so long and far
With little to show than a belly pot?
Well, but I loved and went to war,
The war was won, the love was not.

You think it depends on what you choose.
You better think again, baby,
And heed the Reincarnation Blues:
Fate does the choosing, and I don't mean maybe.

Reincarnation Blues
Canto III

A picture of Evita wreathed in flowers
Adorns the bus's runny windshield.
The driver in his mirror glowers
At the Pampa's wind-blown field.

A line of passengers waits to board,
School kids, tired workers poor.
And there she is, praise the Lord,
To salve my soul, evermore.

Sure, on a teacher's miserable salary
She's poor like the rest, but not as poor
in the soul, or mind if you prefer contrarily,
But she'll now be poor nevermore.

The seat she takes is next to mine.
she opens a copybook to correct the errors
In ink-blotted papers one at a time,
Trying to make sense of the leaning letters.

I little doubt we've known each other
In a past paradise-like life:
As a brother, lover or even mother,
Either of these would define my delight.

I ask – although I already knew --
If she was a teacher in a country school.
The question to her was hardly new:
She nods politely, though kinda cool.

"In the next town", as she erasing rubs,
Leaving little time to make my pitch:

Come live with me and be my love
I quote as we roll around a ditch.

She stands and smiles a smile so fair:
"My English is not so good," she says.
Once outside in the dusty square
To a big guy's kiss she answers yes.

And pointing at my balding dome,
The old lecher still seated here,
Who propositioned her with a poem.
They laugh out loud and rude, I fear.

Let me give you a piece of advice
If it's not already too late to choose.
As a lesson I can't be more concise:
Give heed to the Reincarnation Blues.

Reincarnation Blues
Canto IV

Meditating on the mother of questions,
(I don't mean the coronavirus
Or the First Class Esoteric Lessons)
But the one that necessarily concerns us:

Sooner or later you'll want to know
If life has meaning and if so: what?
We can start be presuming the answer is: no!
If that's the case are we alive or: not?

Or are we actors in a computer game
As the movie Matrix wonkly warned?
Like death itself it's all the same:
No one emerges wholly unharmed.

But if life – human life I mean –
Is real, then so are you and I
Not to mention nature's green
Life of leaves that will also die.

Don't bother going to church
To confess your tawdry trespasses;
It'll surely leave you in the lurch
Cause God doesn't give freepasses.

The killing going on with so much terror
Could make you resort to Brother Booze
But that would be a fateful error
Intones the Reincarnation Blues.

Reincarnation Blues
Canto V

Look at it, if you will, this way:
If you're here now and likely alive,
Where were you before today,
Before, that is, you dropped or dived

Into this wild and woolly world?
Not a cut-rate clue have you
Unless you think you once uncurled
And mewing in Mama's uterus grew.

Well, that's true, but it is not all.
You dew-dropped in like a lonesome lover
From that place you're gonna recall
Once your earthly life is over.

If you don't believe me, wait and see.
no one has ever arrived from nowhere,
Not even The Champ, Mohamed Ali.
The trick now is to find that somewhere.

Stop looking at me with worried wonder
As if I knew who He might be:
The One who'll call with tone of thunder
To searchers yearning to be free.

You'll have to wait for future Cantos,
hopefully in number seven,
Including pathos as well as bathos,
If by then you're not in heaven.

Reincarnation Blues
Canto VI

We'll meet again someday somewhere
The songsters sing, the lovers cry,
As though they knew or even cared,
Forgetting that we all must die,

Some day, somehow, somewhere, some place.
Little do they know it's true
That we all must meet somewhere in space
Although in bodies ever new.

To believe in God is a pretty good start.
To reject him though is also done
By putting the donkey before the cart:
It's not His fault the bad guys won.

You wonder why she died so young
So good, so beautiful, so loved by you,
A love alas not lasting long,
Laced with pain biting through.

I Know, I know, it doesn't seem fair
Perhaps it isn't, but who are we
To Judge? Who are we to care?
Time is long or short, you see.

It's time to stop and dry your tears,
There's nothing more to win or lose,
At least not now as the ending nears:
So rules the Reincarnation Blues.

Reincarnation Blues
Canto VII

You want to live to a ripe old age,
But rather not by growing old.
Can't be done so tether your rage,
Relax, be smart, come in from the cold.

Join the toothless-talking droll,
Balding braggarts who roll the dice
And hesitate to sell their soul
(To you-know-whom) at any price.

Something I almost forgot (on purpose):
Not made and sold by Big Pharma,
Likely as lively as a three-ring circus:
Yours and yours alone: it's karma!

Nothing is forgotten, my friend,
Nothing forgiven without repentance;
No matter how hard you try to bend it
There's no confounding karma's ascension.

Reincarnation Blues has a drumbeat ,
A rhythm that keeps your blood awake.
To challenge it results in a drab defeat,
A sudden sodden chilly checkmate.

Whether you're black or white or in-between,
Your attack is obvious or by a queenly gambit,
It depends on how by the gods you're seen
To have loved – truly or merely faking it.

Reincarnation Blues
Canto VIII

According to John *In the beginning was the Word*
And the Word was with God and the Word was God.
Makes no sense, not at first nor at third.
Sorry sweetheart, but the truth is hard.

The Greeks lacked articles indefinite
Like for example the diminutive "a"
So for them the sense was definite:
And the Word was "a" god - still today.

So Jesus was a guy who today we'd call cool
Who hung out with a wrung-out wrong kinda crowd,
And Pontius Pilate wasn't nearly as cruel
As those who blessed Him with a thorny crown.

He washed his hands, which was no excuse
For killing the Word who Jesus became,
Who suffered crucifixion's abuse,
For many of the mob a death of shame.

What He was trying to convince us of
Was not to obey the bidding of bosses,
but to do our best to be free and to love,
For without love there are darker forces.

When the Church became a royal flush
The inquisitors paved the way to freedom
For them! Not necessarily for us.
What in God's name is the royal rush?

The Reincarnation Blues was not being sung,
But its singing soul was soon in gestation.
For all styles of song start out young
And pass through a period of incubation.

Reincarnation Blues
Canto IX

Often I try to analyze
the reasons for being here and now,
today, kicking and alive,
swearing and forgetting my solemn vow.

Once I was nothing, a bare-ass nude,
and in not too many years to go
again a nothing nada dude.
That's the way it goes, you know.

Once there was no me in view
Till one day there suddenly was
So you ask: what else is new?
To ask is easy, everyone does.

My heart (the know-it-all) disagrees,
and throbbing in feeling-thought decrees
that during the past as a daring dude
I existed, albeit, frankly, crude.

Two-legged, striving, sweating me,
and tomorrow or a little longer maybe,
I'll be back to meet you there where
we once loved, if you still care.

Don't ask where, you'll know where when
Woody the woodpecker riffs a beat
on an old oak tree in a Grecian glen:
Reincarnation Blues doesn't cheat.

Reincarnation Blues
Canto X
(The Brothers Karamazov – a review)

Ivan was an atheist of sorts.
Not that he denied God's existence,
He didn't know about that of course,
But he openly displayed to Him resistance.

How, he asked, could a good-guy God
Allow children to suffer so,
Tortured, abused, the whole nine yards,
Denied even a loving hello?

Alyosha his brother on the other hand
Deeply believed and prayed a lot.
God to him was good and grand.
He loved us all and doubted not.

Mitka though was a hot-headed lot,
Loved Katya and Grushenka as well
With a passion so pure and burning hot
That he landed in a holy hell.

Ivan, therefore, was adept at thought,
Mitka controlled his feeling not,
Alyosha's will evil fought
Without asking where or what.

Philosophers wonder, like any people,
If evil is the absence of good,
Or good inversely is the absence of evil.
Reincarnation Blues knocks wood.

Reincarnation Blues
Canto XI

Proof of God is in the hexagon,
It's not at all like the pentagon.
If you don't believe me, see the bee,
whose brain is smaller than a pea.

It never went to school to learn
the best way to make a hive
and yet its six-sided cells all yearn
to keep the baby-bees alive.

The other gon is the pentagon
whose five-sided wall well protects
the military-industrial-capitalist-complex:
It's what back home we'd call a con.

Proof of Mephisto is in the pentagon,
not at all like the hexagon.
If you don't believe me, see the waste-land:
the bodies burned and buried in sand.

The bee doesn't know what a hexagon is,
it worships the queen and gently gropes her;
he'd gladly give one if he knew how to kiss,
as a royal drone he enjoys her chamber.

Just a word of warning, friend:
If you believe that God's improbable,
when life is over and you're at the end,
He may consider *you* improbable.

Faith, Hope and Love is the way to go,
step by step or all at once.
Hum Reincarnation Blues, then you'll know;
and that, friend, is not a hunch.

Reincarnation Blues
Canto XII
Love's Lament

My sister Faith was first to go,
Her blood was staunched and ceased to flow.
Never was she the worldly type,
And won't return till the time is ripe.

My other sister's name is Hope;
Never was she one to mope.
Her eyes, once fawn's, now sadly droop,
She walks with an ancient's wary stoop.

Hard it will be to linger on
When blissful sister Hope is gone.
Retreating then, I'll take cover,
Waiting for my constant lover.

A generation will rise and when
My sisters will be born again,
They'll care too much not to persist,
Hope's trembling lips insist.

We three will roam the world's wide web
Repeating what the Savior said;
We'll cast away our mourning clothes
And leave them where the wild rose grows:

Being heard above the din,
Calling out and drawing in,
Welcoming the circling dove,
Honoring the name of Love.

The Evil One will be here too,
Our waking giving him the cue
His wicked efforts to redouble.
The World will groan: toil and trouble!

Surely too few will we three be.
Faith, Hope and Love agree
That human help is needed sorely,
That gods alone must prosper poorly.

Christ Comes to Skopelos

Christ consents to be called
To Skopelos
One Easter Sunday
Several years before his year
Two-thousand.

They'd been calling him continually
In all their white-walled
Icon-laden churches,
Never expecting he'd hear their songs.

He heard but will come instead
To a hill above the town
Where a donkey grazes
And cypresses stand in rows
Like green flame.

No one will see him
No one will hear him
When Christ consents to be called
To Skopelos
One Easter Sunday still to come.

Christ came to Skopelos
One Easter Sunday
Several years before his year
Two-thousand.

They'd been calling him relentlessly
In all their white-walled
Icon-laden churches,
Never expecting he'd hear their chants.

He heard, but came instead
To a hill above the town
Where a donkey grazes still
And cypresses stand in rows
Like green flame.

No one saw him,
No one heard him
When Christ came to Skopelos
One Easter Sunday not so long ago.

The Three is One

Forward

Taking my son to the Collegium Musicum
Is good for his musical future, no doubt;
For me it has advantages, too:

The hour and forty minutes spent
Waiting at the sunny outdoor cafe
Give me a chance to think and watch.

The bow-tied, black-vested waiter
Brings my cafecito without
being told - and sweet cookies.

The unkempt park across the street,
The flower-printed tablecloths,
Sunglasses in winter, women in jeans,

Trains passing (newly privatized),
The kiosco "Revistas - Diarios",
Men smoking, uninhibited here.

I light my pipe, puff blissfully,
My thoughts contain the past, no
Avoiding that, the future less

Suppressed. What's uppermost is now.
If life is all and this is happiness,
How on earth can death be less?

If life is all, then this is all
And death is all, it follows.
Such thoughts were once reserved

For the philosopher's dreary den,
Here they stoop to invitations
From cafe idlers, now and then.

The First Circle

A young woman passes my table,
pretty thing with long dark hair
cut abruptly down her back,

Shoulder bag, jeans, enigmatic smile.
Fifty years from now she'll ask
why she did what she did

and wonder what's next on the agenda.
She'll even know it'll soon be over.
Maybe centuries on from now

She'll sit pensive at a cafe table,
see me passing by and wonder
who I am and we'll close a circle,

one of three.

The Second Circle

A boy waits for the waiter to go
Then darts through the noonday traffic.
Black dilated eyes are fixed

on each patron, bare arm extends
a stubby nail-bitten hand.
The tanned man sees only the hand,

doesn't look up from his paper, shakes
his leonine head: no, no.
Two women in fur ignore

the hand, the eyes, the begging boy.
He comes to me. I've read too
that such as he are exploited by

their masters and giving makes it worse.
I don't know, it may be true,
but what is truth in ignorance?

I give him a peso anyway
in case some day the roles reverse
and I'll be he and he'll be me.

A circle is closed, the second of three.

The Third Circle

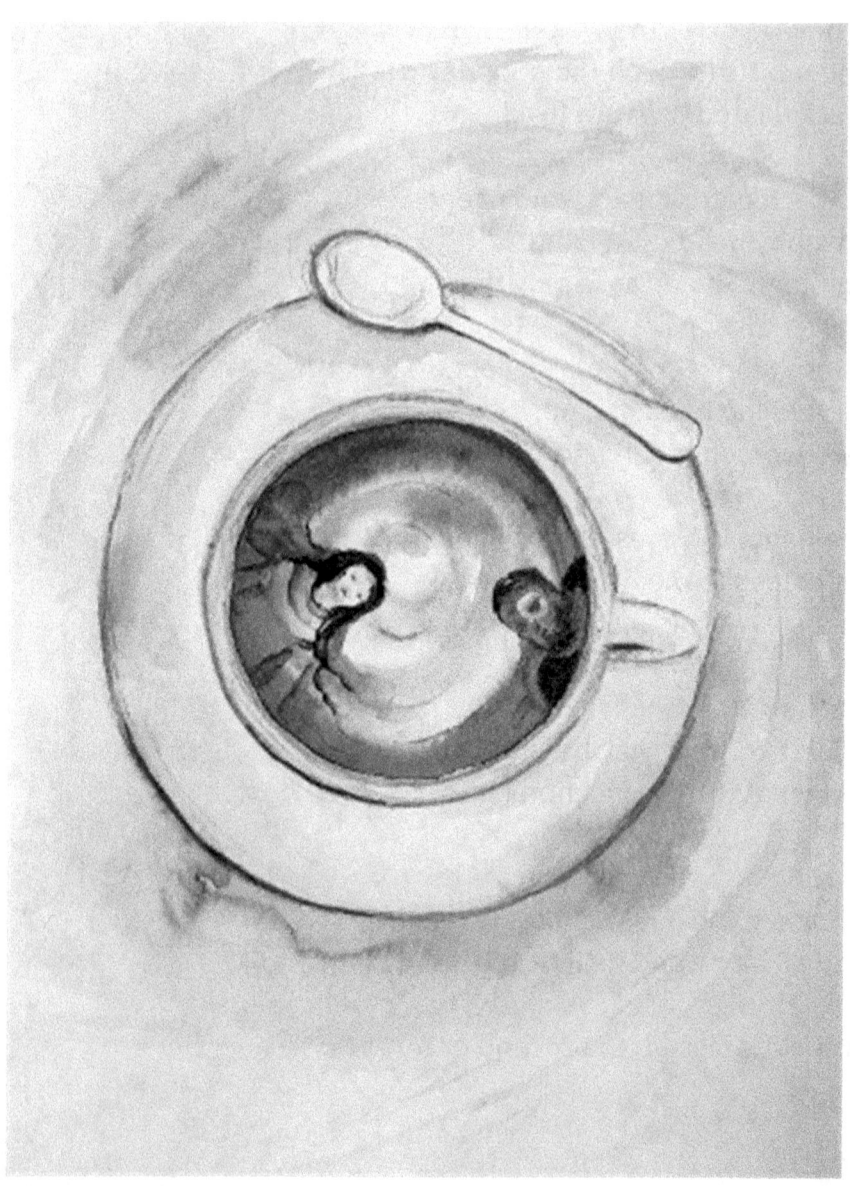

The earth is round, more or less,
As are the heads on our shoulders.
My coffee cup, from the bird's-eye view,

Is round and two-dimensional.
The universe seems to have
The shape of an infinite bubble.

Is this what makes the world go round?
No, it's not enough, this observed,
partly thought-out rotundity.

The unexpected blow, the theft,
The unknown assassin's thrust,
The smiling traitor's perfidious lie

All smudge the portrait's splendor.
An imponderable upsets the equation:
She rounds the corner and looks about.

Like a lost child in a fairy fable
She makes her way to my shaded table.
And takes her place across from me,

For love is an ellipse and the three is one.

The Actress

I watched her cross a lighted stage,
Laugh, groan, weep and rage.
I sat in the darkness of the viewer
With a hundred more, maybe fewer.

She played an aging Southern Belle,
A role which, the truth to tell,
Didn't suit her very well.
Though she had an acting knack,
The fact is she was ... well ... black.

Despite that flagrant contradiction,
Her cultivated Brooklyn diction
And unrelenting youth - nevertheless,
The actress was a great success.

From that night on nothing I spoke,
Ate, wore, did or wrote,
Nothing in fact I even thought
Was unconjoined to what I sought
Most in the world - it's easy to guess:
Her heart, her soul, her passionate caress.

These came in time, and finally went,
As all things worth the striving do.
Fate is known never to relent
And true hearts are distressingly few.

Bad Advice

Times, my friend, are changing,
Rhymes, old boy, are ending,
Clocks all tick your name,
Wines all taste the same.

Letter-writer, blot your tears,
No mail's arrived for you in years.
Walk no somber streets unlit,
Wear nothing that doesn't fit.

Private property's still secure,
Debts will never make you poor,
Nets will always snare their fish,
Lovers are sure to kiss and kiss.

The Mets will rise again,
We only don't know when,
The rains will come again
And so will Brother Ben.

Don't go out if you can help it,
Or you're sure to get a ticket;
Keep your boots on tight,
Don't make love all night.

Deplore the fornicators,
Doomsday indicators,
Begetting beggars, they say,
In a most deplorable way.

Never vote for change,
Prometheus rechain,
Ignore the mysterious call,
Forget them one and all.

Remember, she loves you not,
Remember, you need her not,
Shoot before you're shot –
Whether it's right or not.

Midnight Christmas

The midnight air was a crystal vise
Crushing a billion bits of ice –
One stood out grand and glaring.
Mary, a virgin in her bearing,
Joseph trying to make the best
Of expectations. You know the rest:

Denied the use of house and table,
The birth took place in a humble stable.
Shepherds, black and yellow kings,
The sky a feast of angels' wings.
Thirty years later came the dove,
Ushering in the age of love.

The Initiation

We stood in a circle listening
To the creaking of the boards,
We dared not say a word out loud
For fear of offending the lords.

Three hours full in the circle we stood,
Forbidden to move or speak;
Silence was wrapped in a silken shawl,
Except that the boards did squeak.

The hooded lords then passed among us
And gave us all our rings,
The silken shawl was flung away
And fluttered angels' wings.

Carioca Crack

The ragged sulking boy,
a dark reflection of man,
stands beneath the traffic light,
which changes to amber, then red.
The first cars pass,

the smoking buses never stop for red.
We of the second wave brake and halt,
headlights averted,
eyes straight ahead,
hooded, inverted.

The scruffy snot-nosed kid
limps from car to closed car,
asking for "something"
with pleading hand and eyes.
I look around cautiously

before opening the window a crack,
careful to avoid his grimy hand,
scarred, alive with germs,
and hand him some coins.
The light turns green!

We gun ahead from a standing start
and I lean smugly snugly back,
the only one it would seem
to open up his stingy heart,
If only by a crack.

Chess and Cheese in Crete

To sit outdoors in Crete
with you and coffee, hard toast,
creamy butter and yogurt
after a morning swim
in the rosy-fingered dawn ...

And for lunch at the bubbling port
unidentifiable sea-things,
lukewarm vegetables, cheese,
the deceptive yellow wine
churning my middle-aged blood,

In our room on the creaky bed
with the shutters open wide,
a window on the sea,
your hard nipple swelling,
myself ready to rush ...

One day a thoughtful Arab,
on folding up his tent
under the desert stars,
was touched by the God of chess
and invented that worthy game.

I ask (silently, my love)
how far we are from that country,
and do we care, now,
as I penetrate your darkness
and mate your castled queen.

Found and Lost in Crete

The wind swept your body as it sweeps the world
My love, and I watched you.
The roiling water rushed and brought you back
My love, and I touched you.

The contoured cliffs framed your head at sunset
My love, and I kissed you.
The warm sand ran through your puzzled fingers
My love, and I loved you.

Before my sorrowed eyes the island sank
My love, and I lost you.

The Daughter of the Sun

The Daughter of the Sun
The Mother of the Moon
Taught us all we know,
First she forged the licking fire,
The greatest gift of all,
And showed us how to forge it evermore.

The stone ax to chop and cut and kill,
Baskets woven of high dry grass,
Pots scooped from earth and kilned in fire.
She taught us all we know
The Daughter of the Sun,
The Mother of the Moon.

One day she cooked a soup of river fish.
The flames roared and the pot flowed over,
Soup and fish doused the fire.
Angered by her fate,
The Daughter of the Sun,
Squatted over the embers and pissed a lake.

The fire's dying embers singed her pubic hair,
The burnt vaginal odor engulfed the world,
Kindling desire for woman in us all.

Returning to the underworld
She taught us how to die.
Daughter of the Sun,
Mother of the Moon.

Exile's End

My faraway home is a land of lovers.
A greeting there is no touch of the hand,
No nod of the head, no *Guten Tag, Herr* ...
In that distant land my friends all embrace me
And kiss me and tell me: *Estás en tu casa*.
A cleansing wind blows in from the Pampas,
It swirls even now in the streets of my mind.

In exile I am from this place and that,
So let me tell you a thing I have learned:
All men are exiles and heavy of heart,
The price of a ticket to their ancestral home
Requires a lifetime of arduous travel.
I dare to assume, along with the rest,
That exile won't last much longer than death.

The Expatriate

The problem with most foreign lands
is that they're much too far away,
like the bleachers in Ebbet's used to be
before the debacle of technology.
Also, either they're terribly bland,
foggy, windy and damp, or,
if southerly, downright dangerous,
where bullets fly and sunscreen 21
can't ward off the assassin sun.

Why, then, does he dwell,
ducking and frying, far from the patria
he tearfully invokes over juice of the grape
at a sidewalk table of the corner taberna?
Call it if you will, with a shrug, "escape".
He'll smile and wave away a fly
or toss aside some graying hair
from his glabrous suntanned brow.
"Could be," he mutters, "but who cares now?"

Loneliness is livelier in a distant land,
Be it ever so infuriatingly bland.
But why does it have to be so goddam far,
As distant lands inevitably are?
The answer applies both near and far,
Accessible if the door is left ajar
To contemplate the delight brimming over
In the smirking smile of the expat lover.

He'll bid goodbye to you and,
sandal-clad as once Ulysses,
his uncashed pension check
snug against his bony chest,
walk along the winding lane
home to his dark-tressed mistress
who waits with kisses and a wanton caress.

Foreign lands are far away,
it's true, but so is the expatriate.

Falú in Zurich

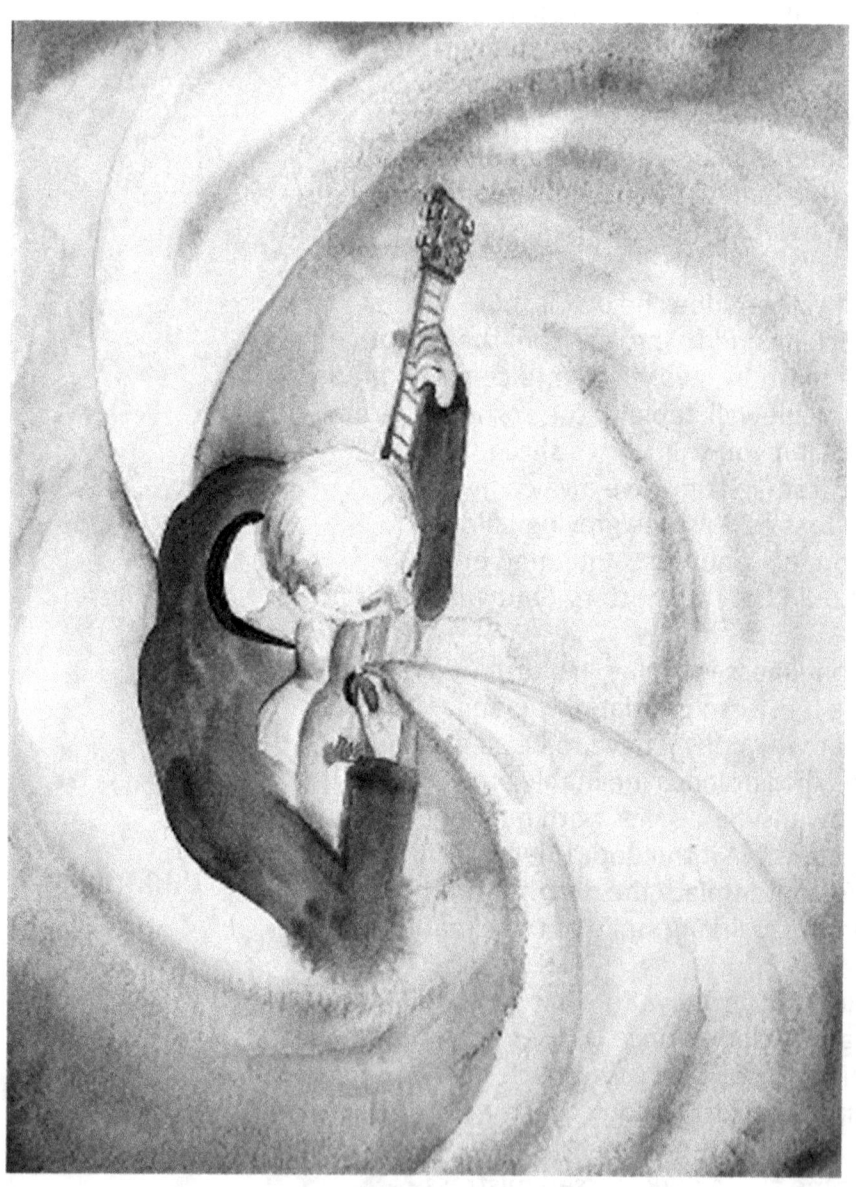

You are a tall man, Falú, and strong,
the guitar is like a flower in your hands,
fingers darting like dragonflies over the strings,
bald head gleaming in the theater lights,
craggy face without emotion.
But you hold the guitar across your breast
and play as though beating your heart.
What are you telling us, Falú?

with songs like *Aires Sureños*, *El Cóndor Pasa*, *Vidalita*?
What do they really mean, Falú?
You don't know yourself, but we,
the hunted and the exiled, we hear you,
Falú, we hear you well.

The Return of the Gaucho

Gracefully the gaucho galloped through
The pampa's waving windswept grasses;
From time to time he stroked his beard,
Black as the eyes of the country's lasses.

Orion patiently made its rounds,
Dripping dust in the River Plate,
While over the *rancho*, his destination,
The Southern Cross guarded the gate.

Three long days and three long nights
The gaucho galloped across the plain,
Resting only when his heaving horse
No longer could stand the strain.

The midnight pampa was ghostly gray,
Starlit by a million sources;
The gaucho flicked the deadly blade,
His mind rehearsed virile curses.

If his woman had loved another man
During his years of abstinence,
He'd kill them both with a silent stroke
And later think of penitence.

Then, like a matchbox tossed aside,
Appeared ahead his home, unchanged
Since he left it for the wars;
He spurred his horse like one deranged.

The *rancho* door fluttered open
Flinging out a flare of light;
A woman trembled on the threshold
Straining to see through the night.

"Juan?" she called in a husky voice
Laced with dregs of hope and dread.
The gaucho flung his knife away,
And bowed his shaggy head.

He prayed that God would forgive his folly,
And thanked the myriad stars above
For having survived the wounds of war,
And having no cause to kill his love.

The Last Judg(e)ment

I'd like to be told infallibilis,
I'd like to be sure when I leave:
Does judg(e)ment applies to all of us,
Or only to those who believe?

Another detail that's worrying,
A matter of weighty import:
Should e follow g sans dissembling,
The way, as a child, I was taught?

Parenthetical - insists the Thesaurus,
As do the grammarians in chorus.

The truth, as you now suspect it,
Has nothing to do with spelling.
The thief comes when least expected,
With or without your compelling.

But I'd like to know for certain,
Yes I'd like to be sure when I leave:
Do the parentheses prophesy curtains
Or not, as my bent's to believe?

Libra

A frantic hand beats the air
Signaling firmly: Stop, No,
Come no closer, Don't you dare!
A shadow falls across one eye,
Commingling with the pungent smoke,
Turning darkness into light
In one decisive stroke.

A familiar smile gives the lie
To previous protestations saying:
Come, come closer still
And taste my ripe delights.

Mireya

Beyond the highest, Aconcagua's peak,
Lives a lady of delicate health
Known by the name Mireya.

Her glance, her smile, her self are all I seek,
Are more to me than worlds of wealth,
The ailing lady Mireya.

Her pace is slower now, embraces weak,
So I will pray for her in stealth,
For the life of my dear Mireya.

*

The friend she was from a distant land,
Beyond Aconcagua's peak.
She knew her time was short ... she took my hand
In hers - she had no need to speak.

The lover from a distant land was she
Whose love was true, and now she's gone away
With me, she said, inside her ... I tried to be
as close, so close: she wanted me to stay.

Her lovely land was distant though,
A strip beyond Aconcagua's peak,
I arrived late, so I'll never more know
Her glance, the smile I used to seek.

The Oak

My branches stretch to all horizons,
My crown touches the circling clouds.
A songbird perches on my steepled terrace
Till the autumn wind warns her off
And sucks my brittle leaves away.
The light from the window's watchful eye
Stares at the night's winter season
And waits, pondering the reason.

If I were the oak before my window,
My crown touching the melting rainbow,
My branches stretching to every horizon,
Providing perches for birds to land on
Until the north wind blows them south
And turns my brittle leaves aglow ...

But I am the presence praying within.
The light from my window's watching eye
Stares at the season's wintry skin
And searches for the reason why
I'm not the oak before my window
Instead of the presence praying within.

Occult Science

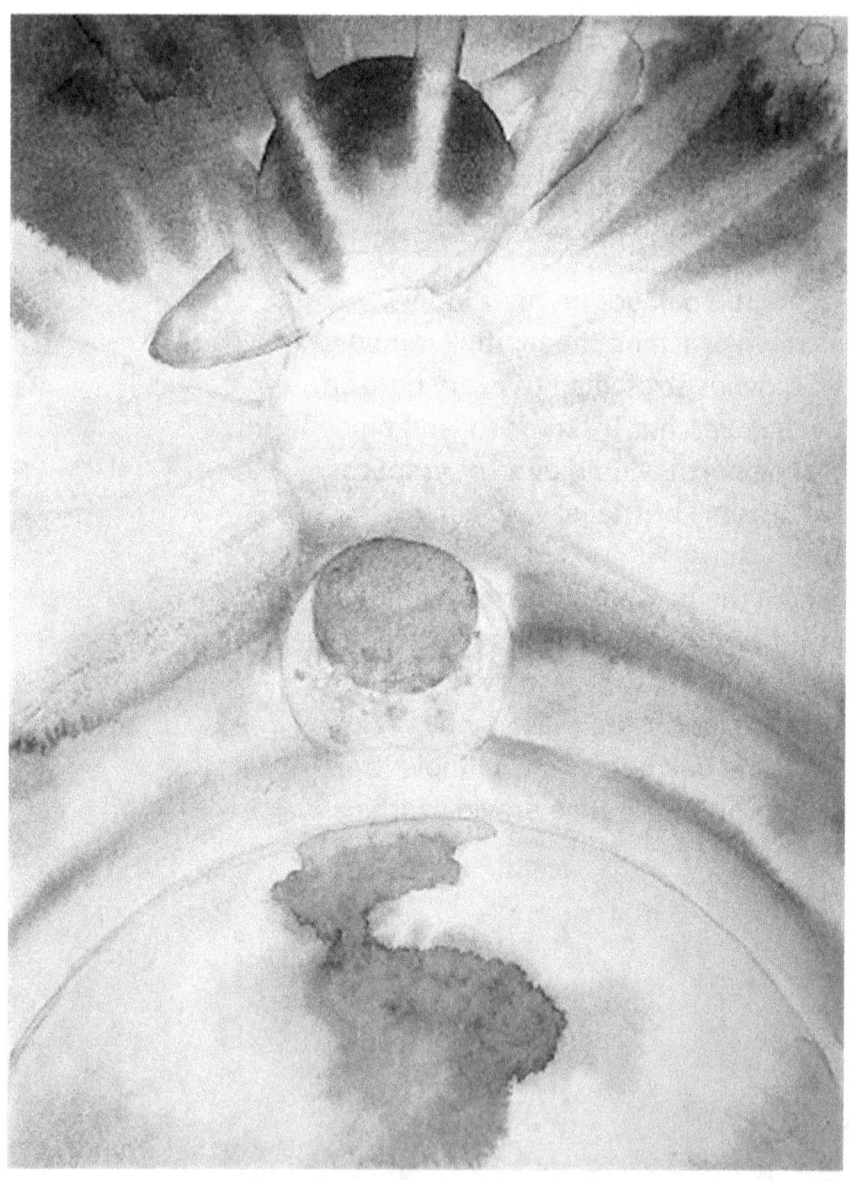

In the beginning was Saturn,
invisible heat, bodies of will.
It died.

Then came Sun, hot and bright,
our bodies became alive.
It died.

Third was Moon, liquid light
and warm, awash with wisdom,
our bodies dynamic.
It died.

To Earth we descended in fire
touched by the Spirits of Form,
rebelled, were expelled,
and wander in exile still.
It will die in love and live again

As Jupiter, Moon reborn,
and die.

Venus will reign victorious
as a Sun more glorious,
and in glory die.

With Vulcan, the seventh kingdom,
the circle closes as spirit.

Old Friends

Six months merely since his birth,
Yet he calmly views the earth
As something precious he once knew
From another point of view.
His wise old eyes are bright and clear,

His smile is happy, gone his tear
As mother reaches down to play.
Old and frequent friends are they,
Longer far than half a year.
Have they held each other dear.

The Parting

A window flew open clattering wood,
A girl leaned out as far as she could.
The gentle breast that filled her dress
Palpitated as from some stress.

A moment later on the bottom floor
A man flung open the rotting door.
She cried: "¿Cuándo volverás?"
"That", he spat, "I know not".

He limped across the puddled street,
Cursing the slowness of his feet.
I've often wondered but never learned
If that man ever returned.

The Pickpocket

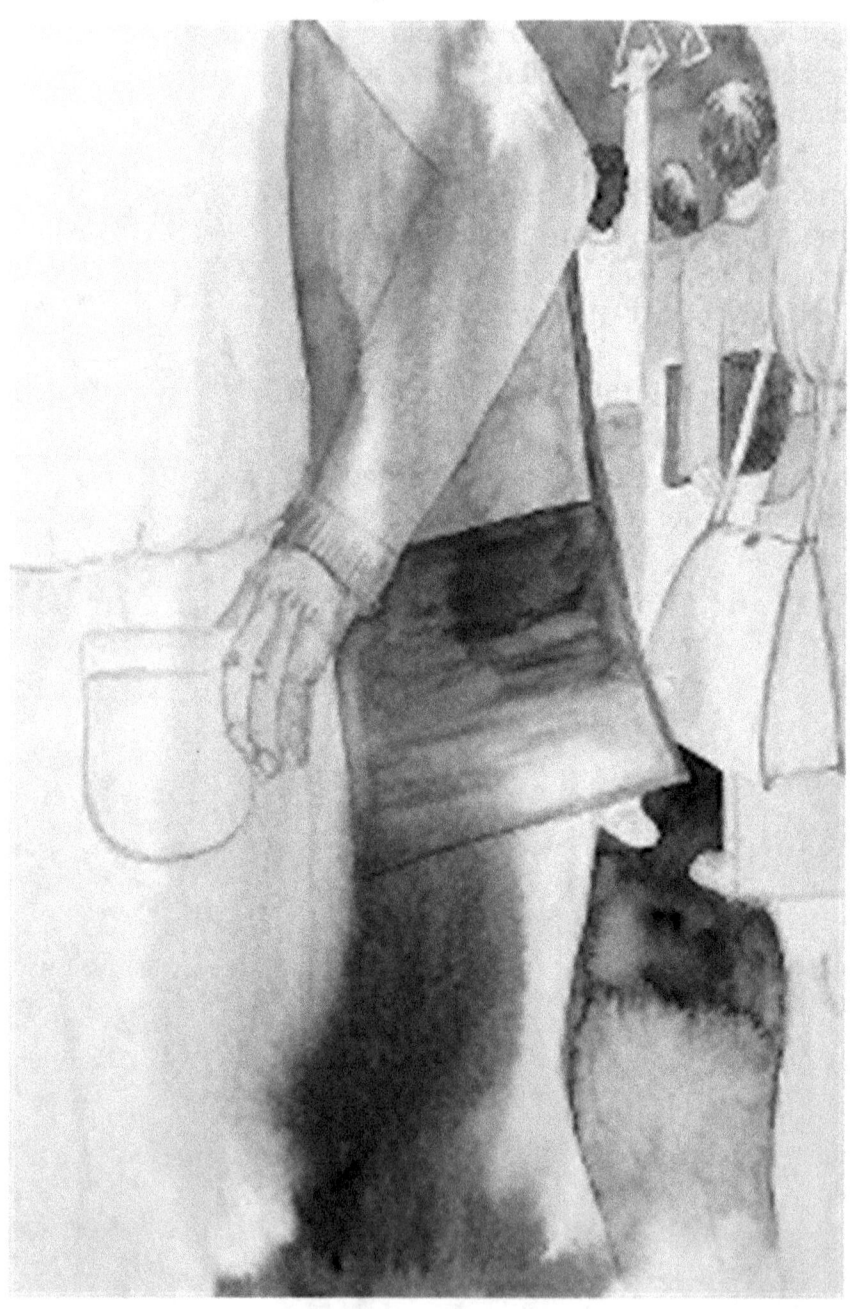

Nostalgia for sleep
Invades the multitude
winding down to the metro.

Then, underground,
standing in rows
with arms upraised

like statues of liberty,
through half-closed lids
they envisage slumber.

Only the pickpocket,
fleet fingers fleecing,
is wide awake.

The Professor of Philosophy

Insists that evil doesn't exist,
It's merely the absence of good.
Killing isn't murder most foul,
But only the absence of letting live.
Hate wouldn't be quite so nasty
If only there were more to love –
Says the Professor of Philosophy.

Only ... what if it's the other way around
And evil's a screw-tailed devil
Whispering in the philosopher's ear,
And it's good that doesn't exist,
Being merely the absence of evil?

Luckily God is much too busy
Continuing His work of creation,
Despite the philosopher's insistence,
To discuss with us His dubious existence.

Sonnet to Love

I'm free to love someone who doesn't love me,
I'm just as free to hate someone who does;
That suffering attaches to both is easy to see,
A suffering as cruel as any there ever was.
Why it is so is purely academic,
To ask is not the purpose of this piece,
I only know the disease is epidemic,
Incurable with normal means at any price.
If the love of her who loves me well
To her who doesn't could somehow be applied,
A solution of sorts it would constitute, but hell
For her who loves me, whose love had not yet died.
Then let me love them both and all the rest,
A costly choice, but probably the best.

The Tall Trees of Brooklyn

Tall are the trees of Brooklyn.
The kids don't know their names,
Except for the chestnut
Which drops its shiny fruit
On rain-washed sidewalks.

They stand in tiny plots
Little larger than their trunks,
Their roots spread deep and wide
Beneath concrete blankets,
Holding the city together.

The kids gaze down car-lined streets
To where the tall trees
End their march.
They don't know their name,
But they love them all the same.

Missing The Point

Galloping on the circumference
on mounts that never trip
or hesitate amidst revolutions,
we soon arrive where we started –
missing the point.

Inside the circle glows the point,
once I reined up and looked:
It glowed and spun around
like a puppy chasing its tail
happy I'd stopped and watched,
and grew to infinite size.

All the stuff of the world it contained,
from Adam the First to Adam Smith,
and finally to Frank T. Smith,
year by year, day by day,
arriving finally at today.

I blinked and for an infinite moment
all the joy liquid and brimming,
from Eve to Magdalena,
from my mother to my daughter,
burning bright blinded me.

I turned away
and spurred my mount,
daring not to stay for fear
of viewing the fearsome future –
and missing, still, the point.

The Return of the Magi

This town is one we've seen before:
These crooked lanes, that stable door,
Although it must have been a dream,
For never were we here before.

And that quick dog, scared and lean,
Crossing the square scarcely seen
And the dark-haired girl leaning out
The hostel window familiar seem.

The sky was lit by the evening star
As now, but brighter then by far;
Above us shuddered angels' wings
And we had journeyed far, so far.

Celestial Traffic Jam

The atmosphere's crowded
with the rushing souls
of the dearly departed
on their way to the stars
and other destinations.

Others glide silently down
to try again an earthly life
hopefully better than the last one
wishing to arrive before it's late.
Not leaving everything to fate.
Two-way traffic creates a jam
at the intersection *Moon*.
Birth on earth it seems,
though of dubious avail,
hasn't lost its attraction.

The Working Stiff

You were a working stiff then
in a free market world – when
hungry you were, cold and wet,
cheated of all except your sweat.

You hoped for insurrection,
you dreamed of resurrection.
Then they told you about where
those bad guys were over there.

To fight for your country you ought,
Which sounded right so you went and fought.
You didn't know then that you fought
for it – the market force.

You died and your blood ran red
down a foreign riverbed.
Some of you came back then
as working stiffs again
– and –
hungry you are, cold and wet,
cheated out of even your sweat.
No talk now of resurrection
or even insurrection.

At last you know it's late:
A fuckin' robot's who you hate
You asshole stiff sans work,
in this free for the market world.

Someday things will change you hope,
you'll have what you need to live a life
without having to hang from a rope.
An angel will come to cut with a knife ...

Stop it! you worthless working dope.
No angel's gonna come to help.
Only you, once woken up
can cause the crushing ice to melt.

So, round up your brothers and sisters, yeah!
Together your voices can vote a decree,
something that's true but very rare:
that peace needs love and love is free.

Ultimate Questions

go nowhere
Like answers to questions unasked.
They lean on lamp-posts in whipping wind,
They shiver and raise their collars high.
Ah, but the humble query –
About how to plane a knotty board
Or the grade of oil in your crankshaft,
The tie to match a new jacket
Or the perfume to wear to your prom:
They are really and readily asked
And never retire unanswered
Like quote What is truth? unquote.

It was left unanswered then,
So what would be the point
Of asking once again.

Twin Pillars of Wisdom

The world turned in its usual round
A splendid dawn in pastels gowned.
Then paused ... shuddered ... and shrieked.

The Twin Towers groaned,
Reluctant bombers, unerringly pilots,
Pierced those daunted pillars.

Terribly they tumbled to the ground,
Now rubble burning hot with flesh,
Entangled with bone and death.

Mephisto raised his fist exultant.
To God he cried: *You gave me leave,
Now tell me who has won!*

The Angels wept for the souls they met,
Wandering in know-how's debris,
Not caring where they were bound,

One was stern as he looked around.
Calmly he called to the aimless souls,
Who gathered under his wing.

God heard the cries – Mephisto's too –
And brooded long at the ways of men.
How will it end? he asked of them.

The Drone Cometh

All the people of the village unite
to sing and drink and dance the night;
The bride is lovely in her new white gown
Her smile lights up all the town.

Look out, be careful, the drone is coming,
The time has come to think of running!

All the people so happy and gay
The groom knows not what to say,
The mother of the bride with pride is swollen;
A moment of peace is being stolen.

Look out, be careful the drone is coming,
The time has come to think of running!

The father, worried, offers a toast:
To peace, he says, *and happiness*.
The bridegroom answers with a boast:
Fear not, father, God is near,
Fear not, mother, love is dear.

Look out, the drone is coming soon;
The drone, the drone, it cometh here.
The drone – ka---boom!
The drone – ka---boom! Ka-boom!
Now there's really nothing to fear.

All the people of the village unite
To die together this moonless night.
The bride herself is equally dead,
Her white dress is stained with red.
The mother, the father, toast no more
The bridegroom's head is a mass of gore.

Look out, the drone is coming soon;
The drone, the drone, it cometh here.
The drone – ka---boom!
The drone – ka---boom! Ka-boom!
The drone cometh here.

Translations

Credo

by Leon Felipe

Here I am ...
Still in this world ... old and tired ... waiting to be called.
Often have I wanted to flee through the damned, condemned door,
But an invisible angel touched me on the shoulder and told me severely:
No, the time has not yet come ... you must wait ...
So here I wait ...
In Yesterday's same old suit,
Creating and recalling memories,
Examining my conscience,
Closely scrutinizing my life ...
What a disaster! ... Not a talent! ... I lost it all!
Only my eyes can still cry. That's what's left to me ...
And my hope rises to say in anguish:
The next time I will do better, Lord,
because ... It's true, isn't it, that we are born again?
I believe that God always gives us another life, other new lives,
other bodies with other tools, with other instruments ...
other sonorous boxes in which the immortal, traveling soul can better move,
slowly, very slowly to correct, down the centuries,
our old sins, our obstinate sins ...
thus little by little eliminating the primal poison of our blood, that comes from long ago ...
Time goes by and pulls it all down, transforms it all.
Nevertheless the centuries pass and the soul is elsewhere ... but it **is**!
I believe that we have many lives,
that they are successive purgatories,
and that these successive purgatories, all together,
Constitute hell, the purifying hell,
At the end of which waits the Light, the Great God.
Neither hell ... nor the fire and the pain are eternal.

Only the light burns without respite,
Adamantine,
Infinite,
Merciful,
Enduring forever and ever...
There it is with its divine attributes,
Only my eyes are not capable of seeing it...
These poor eyes that yet can do naught but cry.

Prologue in Heaven
from **FAUST** by Johann Wolfgang von Goethe

Characters
The Lord, the Heavenly Hosts, later Mephistopheles

The Archangels step forward.

RAPHAEL:
The sun resounds as once of old
In loving spheres of motley song,
Predestined is its journey bold,
Ripening as it flows along.
Its sight the angels new strength gives,
Though none can fathom how it's done;
The inconceivable still lives
In glory as when the days were one.

GABRIEL:
How marvelously right
The splendiferous earth revolves,
It interchanges heaven's light
With dismal darkness unresolved,
It churns the seas and violent rivers
through rocky soil in convolution,
and rocks and seas apart are driven
In swift eternal revolution.

MICHAEL:
And storms complete with briny bluster
From sea to land and land to sea,
Forge a chain from fury's fluster
That binds the world in harmony.
A fearful bolt of lightning's flame
Precedes the devastating thunder;

But angels worthy of the name
Revere in awe each daily wonder.

ALL THREE:
Its sight the angels new strength gives,
Though none can fathom how it's done;
The inconceivable still lives
In glory as when the days were one.

MEPHISTOPHELES:
Since you, O Lord, approach us once again
And ask us how our work is getting on,
And since I've given pleasure now and then,
You see me here debating with the throng.
My choice of words leaves much to be desired,
I'm subject to this circle's cruelest scorn;
You'd die laughing at pathos by me inspired,
If laughter were not a thing you'd long forsworn.
About the sun I've nothing to confess,
I only see how men are in a mess.
The god of earth is still his father's son,
As queer as when the days were one.
Somewhat better would he live
Had you forgot heaven's light to give.
His use of reason's minimal,
Lower than the lowest animal,
He seems to be, with permission of Your Grace,
A cricket jumping all around the place,
Who's always spinning and spinning springs,
and in the grass the same old lyric sings;
If only he'd molder in the grass
And not stick his nose in such morass.

THE LORD:
>Have you nothing else to say?
>Must you always arrogance display?
>Doesn't anything on earth seem good to you?

MEPHISTO:
>No Sir, I find things rotten through and through.
>So sorry for humanity am I
>That tormenting it almost makes me cry.

THE LORD:
>Do you know Faust?

MEPHISTO.
>The doctor?

THE LORD:
>My servant.

MEPHISTO:
>Of course. He serves you in a special way,
>Keeping even food and drink at bay,
>Confusion plays the devil with his mind.
>Though knowing only fools would take such measures,
>He asks that heaven show him orbs sublime
>And earth provide him all its pleasures;
>Not all that's high nor all that's low
>Can satisfy his will to know.

THE LORD:
>   Although he serves me in some confusion,
>   I'll gladly show him soon the light.
>   The gardener knows that flowers in profusion
>   And fruit adorn his trees when all is ripe.

MEPHISTO:
>   What will you bet? You'll lose, you know,
>   If me you give permission
>   To lead him where he longs to go.

THE LORD:
>   As long as he's on earth alive,
>   So long it's not to you forbidden.
>   Men must err as long as they still strive.

MEPHISTO:
>   I thank you, Lord. I never kept it hidden
>   That once they're dead I keep my distance,
>   It's rosy cheeks I love in every instance.
>   I'm not at home to corpses in my house,
>   I like to play the game of cat and mouse.

THE LORD:
>   All right, I give you leave to try it.
>   Seduce that spirit from its primal source
>   And guide it, should you find a way to beguile it,
>   Along the fearsome pitfalls of your course;
>   And stand disgraced when finally you admit:
>   A good man, in spite of iniquity's force,
>   Will find the path to truth before he's quit.

MEPHISTO:
>Done! It won't take very long.
>I have no doubt that I will win the bet,
>And when I do, please don't forget the debt,
>Allow my triumph its rightful measure.
>Dust shall he eat, and with pleasure,
>Just like the serpent, my celebrated pet.

THE LORD:
>Even that you're free to try.
>Your kind and you I've never hated,
>Of all the spirits who me deny,
>The rogue by me the least is rated.
>The deeds of men are easily put to sleep,
>They love their undisturbéd rest.
>That's why I give them over to his keep,
>Who as the devil puts them to the test.
>But you, true sons of God, enjoy
>The living wealth of beauty's joy.
>Let Being – active and alive forever –
>Embrace you in love's delightful folds.
>Make fast the things that swerve and sever
>With thought that steadfast holds.

MEPHISTO:
>I enjoy seeing the Old Man now and then
>To make sure our rapport is never broken.
>It's damned decent of Himself once again
>In person with the Devil to have spoken.

About the Author

Frank Thomas Smith is an American expatriate, born and bred in Brooklyn, New York, who has lived in Europe (Switzerland, Germany) and South America (Argentina) for many years. He has been active in international commercial aviation, education (Waldorf) and consulting. He is now a translator and author. He resides with his wife in the Traslasierra Valley in Argentina. He is the editor and publisher of www.SouthernCrossReview.org.

OTHER BOOKS
authored or translated by
Frank Thomas Smith
All titles available at Amazon.com

ANTHROPOSOPHICAL FANTASIES (by Roberto Fox, as told to Frank Thomas Smith): Anthroposophy, also known as Spiritual Science, is not known for fantastic literature, or fiction at all. So how can stories with titles like "Life on Mars," or "The Girl in the Floppy Hat," or "To Hunt a Nazi" qualify as anthroposophical. They do not — until now. Therefore, this book is groundbreaking. You may smile at times, even laugh; other stories may cause a lump in your throat ...
ISBN: 978-1948302104

ANTHROPOSOPHICAL GUIDELINES (Rudolf Steiner, translated by Frank Thomas Smith): this volume contains a collection of short essays by Steiner for the members of the Anthroposophical Society. They were written near the end of Steiner's life and in a way summarize, in highly concentrated form, the whole of anthroposophy. Each essay ends with a short summary of its contents and these are known, in this translation, as the "guidelines." The guidelines are mantras and can be used quite fruitfully for meditation. Frank Thomas Smith provides a new, reinvigorated translation of Rudolf Steiner's classic, "Anthroposophical Leading Thoughts."
ISBN: 978-1948302418

CORONAVIRUS PANDEMIC II (by Judith von Halle, translated by Frank Thomas Smith): In this book, the main focus is not on the distressing social developments that have arisen as consequence of the coronavirus pandemic – and for good reason: Although there are already (thankfully) many quality descriptions and articles about this complex of problems and questions, at the same time on the other hand a dangerous knowledge-vacuum has arisen. Therefore in this book I will refrain from elaborating on the problems already made widely visible in favor of this knowledge-vacuum, which will be outlined as an addition to what has already been described in Vol. I.
ISBN: 978-1948302357

ESOTERIC LESSONS FOR THE FIRST CLASS Volumes I, II, and III (Rudolf Steiner, translated by Frank Thomas Smith): During the re-founding of the Anthroposophical Society at Christmas 1923, Rudolf Steiner also reconstituted the 'Esoteric School' which had originally functioned in Germany from 1904 until 1914, when the outset of the First World War made it's continuance impossible. Twenty-eight lectures in three Volumes with in-line illustrations and blackboard drawings.
ISBN: 978-1948302289 (vol. 1),
   978-1948302302 (vol. 2),
   978-1948302333 (vol. 3)

FAVELA CHILDREN (by Ute Craemer, translated by Frank Thomas Smith): Ute Craemer is an educator and social worker who has dedicated over fifty years of her life to teaching and nurturing the poor children of the favelas (slums) in Brazil. As an experienced Waldorf teacher, she has been able to understand the needs of the children and their families and provide them with the spiritual nourishment they cry out for. Favela Children is a moving and informative account of Ute Craemer's social work in the favelas and of her personal development ...
ISBN: 978-1948302425

THE HISTORY AND ACTUALITY OF IMPERIALISM (Rudolf Steiner, translated by Frank Thomas Smith): In 1920 Rudolf Steiner had already foreseen that the future imperialism would be economic rather than military or nationalistic. In these three lectures he describes the history of imperialism from ancient times to the present and into the future. The Anglo-American would play an increasingly important role in future developments, so the English visitors who attended must have been especially attentive.
ISBN: 978-1948302203

JOURNEY TO THE STARS (by Frank Thomas Smith): The protagonists of these 12 stories are involved in fascinating adventures, which will delight young readers and leave an indelible impression on their minds and hearts. For children from 9 years old on up.
ISBN: 978-1948302395

LOVE IN THE LIFE OF SPIES is, as its title suggests, a love story between two spies during the Cold War, an East German woman and an American man, each working for their respective opposing clandestine agencies and, therefore, against each other. Their meetings, seemingly accidental, unfold over years in the United States, Germany, Argentina, Paraguay and, finally, serve only to reveal an uncertain future. It asks the question: is such a love viable under such complicated and adverse geopolitical circumstances? Or was it meant to be - at least as a possibility - according to karma's blueprint. The answer, although not definitive, is maybe, or even yes involving, strangely enough, Anthroposophy.
ISBN: 978-1948302517

THE MAGIC MOUND (by Frank Thomas Smith): Sergio and his younger brother, Divino are poor children who live in a favela (slum) in Sao Paulo, Brazil. They go on vacation with their revered teacher, dona Ute (pronounced oo-teh), to the country house of one of Ute's friends. Once there, they leave the house together to fetch kindling wood. They cross a stream and discover a strange round mound surrounded by white stones ... for children from 9 years old on up.
ISBN: 978-1948302258

THE TALKING TREES / LOS ÁRBOLES PARLANTES (by Frank Thomas Smith): Alma and Nico live on opposite ends of a forest near their homes. One day when they are both reading the same book (The Magic Mound) within the forest, but far from each other, the trees suddenly talk to them. A bilingual edition for children from 9 years old on up.
ISBN: 978-1948302715

TOWARD A THREEFOLD SOCIETY (Rudolf Steiner, translated by Frank Thomas Smith): This work, written late in the life of Rudolf Steiner, makes use of a threefold analysis of the human individual and of human society. Man as an individual, or in a group, functions basically in three modes: thinking/perceiving, feeling/valuing, and willing/planning/acting. A unit of functioning, whether a part of an individual or part of a society has its proper role. Each role needs a certain respect from other areas if it is to function properly ...
ISBN: 978-1948302166

www.ingramcontent.com/pod-product-compliance
Lightning Source LLC
Chambersburg PA
CBHW062034120526
44592CB00036B/2097